MOM'S GURU

A GUIDE TO COMPUTERS

BY

DEANNA MORRIS CONWAY

This is a step by step guide I developed for my Mom to meet some of her basic computing needs. If you want to learn the basics of Internet, Email, Copying, Pasting and Downloading Digital Photos, but don't want all of the technical jargon – this is the guide for you. Each process is explained with click by click instructions along with many helpful graphics. There is also a quick start guide in the Appendix for easy reference. You will learn when to left click, right click or double click and many useful shortcuts. There is a second Appendix listing many popular and useful websites.

Table of Contents

4

MOM'S GURU

A GUIDE TO THE INTERNET, EMAIL, COPYING AND PASTING, DOWNLOADING DIGITAL PHOTOS AND MORE

This is a book I started for my mother, to help her to become more confident and comfortable using her new Windows 7 computer. My mother first started using a computer at home to help with her study of our family's genealogy with a Windows version 3.1 computer. She was able to master most of her computing needs using that computer, but it was doggedly slow and finally her three children compelled her to get a newer and faster computer. She hated it. It wasn't the same, it wasn't as easy and she liked the old one better. But Mom is not one to complain, so she adapted to it, like it or not.

She persevered for several years with her Windows Vista computer with just an occasional call for assistance. Most of the time, I could walk her through whatever difficulty she was having over the phone. But there were times when I needed to make a house call. I only thought her first computer was slow. This one was molasses in winter. I told her that she needed to upgrade and that she would love the new Windows 7 operating system. Of course, the thought of a new computer system brought out the stubbornness in her that I thought only my dad could exhibit. This was a side of Mom I had never seen before. Really, she didn't need anything that was faster. What else was she going to do with her time? So each time I was called to look at her computer, I warned my husband in advance that there would be no dinner that night unless it was take out.

But miracles do happen. Miracles with my mother that can only be brought about by my brother – her oldest child – and only son. He made a cross country trip to visit for Thanksgiving in 2010. He is computer savvy in ways that I can only dream about. And he is very patient and accommodating – and a great cook. He took it upon himself to have a look at Mom's computer and see what he could do to speed things up a bit. He fired it up, only to wait, and wait for the start-up process to finish. And he waited some more, and then decided to help mom in the kitchen by chopping cranberries for her wonderful relish while the computer hummed and blinked and came to life. Chopping done, he checked on the progress of the computer, and found that it was ready to go – nowhere. My brother is self employed and to him time is money and her computer was a total waste of both. I got a call from him while I was in the middle of assembling a green bean casserole. He told me that the computer was shot and that Mom needed a new one, and that we were going to the after Thanksgiving Day sales to pick one out for her. I laughed to myself, knowing that this idea of his would never fly. Not with my mom.

Thanksgiving Day arrived and everyone assembled at my house for a great dinner mostly prepared by Mom and my sister, but I still got the credit for hosting and having a clean house. Things were going splendidly, the food was good, wine flowed and our family was together. There were great stories related by my aunt and my dad that had most of us in tears from the laughter. And then the unthinkable happened. Mom whipped out the after Thanksgiving Day sales ads and announced to one and all that she had decided to get a new computer. I almost choked on my pumpkin pie. But I set my alarm for 4:30, and we were able to deliver a new Windows 7 computer to my mother's house before I had to be at work at 8:00 am.

Sadly, my father passed away in February. As we sorted through his military keepsakes and family photos, we thought it would be nice to be able to share them with other family members. My brother and I have undertaken the task of scanning these old photographs and 35 mm slides and posting them on web albums so that they can be shared. While my mother is not new to digital photography, she was thrilled that we could do this and still preserve the original photo in its original format. This got her to thinking about her own digital photos. She said that she was planning to take her memory card from her camera to a local store and have the pictures transferred to a CD that we could load on our computers. We could then view the pictures on a larger scale to be able to decide which ones were worthy of printing.

"That's a great idea, Mom. We can even load them on the web albums and share them. But let me see your memory card and find out what we can do here." I almost hated to show her how easy it is to transfer the pictures from the card to her computer and make her own CD. She was so excited to have asked all the right questions at the photo lab, and she has done a great job of choosing and editing the pictures she does print. But each of those prints, and each of those CD's that she would have made at the photo lab cost much more than what it costs to do the same thing at home.

Fast forward to Easter dinner at my mom's house. I announced that I was planning on writing a book on computers to help Mom and other computer users like her. Mom told me that she doesn't want to read a book to learn how, she wants to learn by doing. I took a look at her computer and noticed all of the sticky notes pasted to the edges of the monitor and how each one was for a different task; saving a file, forwarding an email, printing a web page, and more. But her set of sticky notes was not organized in any particular order and was by no means a comprehensive set of instructions for all of her computing needs.

So now this has become a guide for each task that she wants or needs to do – organized and easy to navigate with click by click instructions each step of the way.

For those who want a quick lesson, there is an appendix with condensed instructions for most of the topics covered in this guide. If there are topics that you want more information about or you want to be able to use available shortcuts, read through the chapters in order, or choose the ones that you need. Let's get started.

THE INTERNET – YOUR WAY

SETTING UP YOUR HOMEPAGE

Power on your computer and ensure that you have a connection to the internet. If you have broadband, cable or satellite, you should be connected automatically. If you have problems, contact your internet service provider and they will be able to walk you through the steps to get connected.

For this book, I will be using programs that come installed on most computers. For internet browsing, most often that program will be Microsoft Internet Explorer.

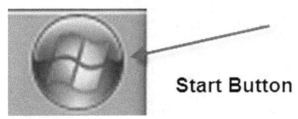

Start Button

Using your mouse, navigate to the START button which is located in the lower left corner of the computer screen. LEFT CLICK ONCE. This will bring up a separate window listing programs and shortcuts that are available. The left side of this window has a white background and lists programs. The right side has a blue background and lists shortcuts to different areas of your computer. In the white section, left click on the ALL PROGRAMS link, look for the program that is listed as INTERNET EXPLORER. Without clicking, move your mouse pointer to INTERNET EXPLORER, it will highlight in blue when you are hovering over it.

LEFT CLICK ONCE.

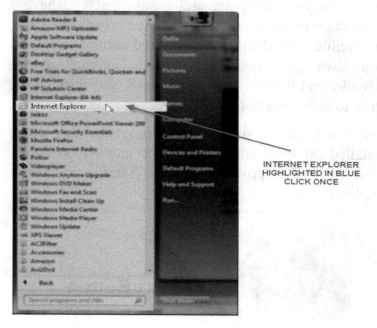

INTERNET EXPLORER
HIGHLIGHTED IN BLUE
CLICK ONCE

A new window will open to a default internet page. Usually it is a page that is associated with your particular brand of computer. You will want to set your internet to open to a page to suit your needs. There are many homepages or start pages available. Some of the more popular ones include; Google, MSN, and Yahoo.

You may have one you that have used previously or one that has been recommended to you. Let's get your homepage set up to open automatically when you start INTERNET EXPLORER.

At the top of the page is a white horizontal address bar. This is where you will type website addresses which you want to view. LEFT CLICK in the address bar.

I have typed in the address for Yahoo, but you can use any address you choose. It is not necessary to type in the **http://.** Just start typing with www. and your address. Now press the ENTER key on the keyboard and your page will load. Look this page over and decide if it is what you want to use for your homepage. Most will offer an area to search and an area that includes current news, sports and weather. If this is the page for you, then you will want to set it as your homepage. To do this you need to find the area below the address bar which is your menu bar. Find the word TOOLS and LEFT CLICK ONCE.

 **TOOLS**

This brings up a menu of available tools. At the bottom of this list is one that says INTERNET OPTIONS.

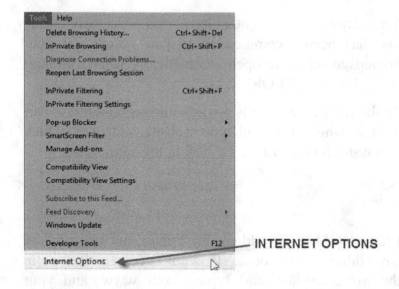

INTERNET OPTIONS

LEFT CLICK ONCE

This opens a new window.

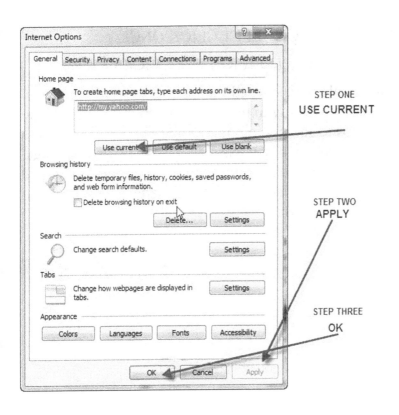

LEFT CLICK ONCE on USE CURRENT button, (you will see the address of the website change to the one you entered for your homepage). LEFT CLICK ONCE on APPLY, then LEFT CLICK ONCE on OK. This will set your homepage so that each time you open INTERNET EXPLORER you will land on your homepage. Go ahead and try it now. Close the internet window by left clicking once on the red X in the upper right corner. Then reopen a new internet window. Here are the steps.

START BUTTON –LEFT CLICK ONCE

INTERNET EXPLORER –LEFT CLICK ONCE

This should have opened the internet to your homepage. You are now ready to browse the internet. You can type any website address into the ADDRESS BAR, and press ENTER on your keyboard to take you to that page. Anytime that you want to return to your homepage, you can left on the icon (picture) of the house on the right side of the toolbar.

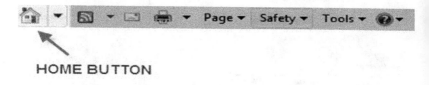

HOME BUTTON

ADDING FAVORITES

As you are browsing the internet, you will no doubt find websites that you like and will want to return to frequently. To avoid having to type in the website address each time, there is a shortcut that you can use to make your favorites available with just one click.

While you are on a site that you want to re-visit frequently, left click on the yellow star located on the left side of the toolbar. LEFT CLICK ONCE on the yellow star with the green arrow to add a special tab that will take you with one click to the website. If you have a lot of favorite sites, this can soon clutter your toolbar area. If this is the case, LEFT CLICK ONCE on the word FAVORITES in the MENU BAR. This will open a sub menu of favorites sites. At the very top of the list is ADD TO FAVORITES. LEFT CLICK ONCE on this to add your site to this list. When you do a new window will open to confirm that you want to add this to your list of favorites.

YOU CAN CHANGE OR SHORTEN THE FAVORITE NAME HERE

Shorten the name to whatever will help you remember it easily. A lot of the names will have descriptions of the website in addition to the name. Then LEFT CLICK ONCE on the ADD BUTTON.

If you don't find some of these bars, move your mouse pointer to the top area of the web page and RIGHT CLICK with your mouse ONCE. This will open a CONTEXT MENU which is pictured below. Check by left clicking to select which menus you want to have available to you. I suggest at the minimum you select the MENU BAR, FAVORITES BAR and the COMMAND BAR. These will give you easy access to many of the tasks that you will use frequently. Select the STATUS BAR, which will be located at the bottom of your web page to see the progress of the website as it loads. I don't really find this necessary as it takes up a bit of the screen and makes the site you are viewing smaller. But if you have a slow connection, you might want to be able to see the progress of the page as it loads. Finally, if you are satisfied with the placement of the toolbars, you can select LOCK THE TOOLBARS, which will keep them from being shifted inadvertently to another location and keep you from searching for them.

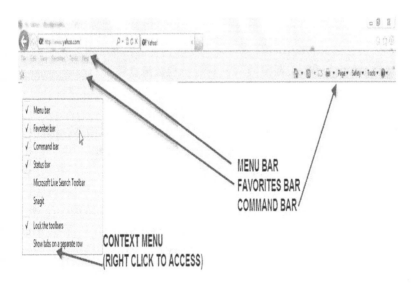

It is worth noting that when you use your mouse, you will generally click once or twice with the LEFT mouse button. This will open a website, program or select an action to perform. When you *RIGHT* CLICK ONCE with your mouse, it will open a context menu if one is available. Inside the context menu, you will need to LEFT CLICK to select an action. You can practice this by right clicking on different areas of websites that you are viewing to see what actions are available. You don't have to choose to do any of the actions, just look over the menu and then move your mouse away and left click to close it. Right clicking can be a valuable time saver and is worth using when you can.

SHORTCUTS AND THE TASKBAR

You will notice at the bottom of your computer screen a horizontal bar with icons (pictures) on the left and perhaps the time and date on the right. This is the TASKBAR. The left side incorporates the START BUTTON and PROGRAM ICONS. The right side contains the NOTIFICATION AREA and to the rightmost is a button to SHOW DESKTOP.

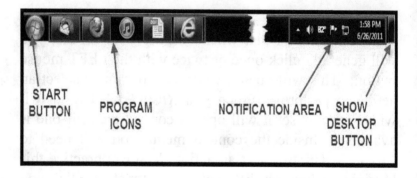

START BUTTON

Left clicking on the start button will give you access to installed programs, search, computer functions and shut down options. Each of these is located in a different area on the start menu as you will see in the graphic on the following page. On the left is the area where your installed programs can be accessed. Just hover your mouse pointer over the words ALL PROGRAMS and the list will expand to show what is available. Below that is an area with a magnifying glass that says SEARCH PROGRAMS AND FILES. By left clicking in this box, you can type what you want, hit enter on the keyboard and the computer will do a search for all programs, files and folders that contain your search information. The right portion of the start menu contains most COMPUTER FUNCTIONS that you will need to use, including quick access to your documents, photographs and music. And finally, below those is an area with the words SHUT DOWN with a right pointing arrow. Left click on this arrow to bring up a menu of available actions. Here you can restart your computer, log off or put the computer to sleep. If you want to power off the computer, you will need to left click on the button with the words SHUT DOWN rather than clicking on the arrow.

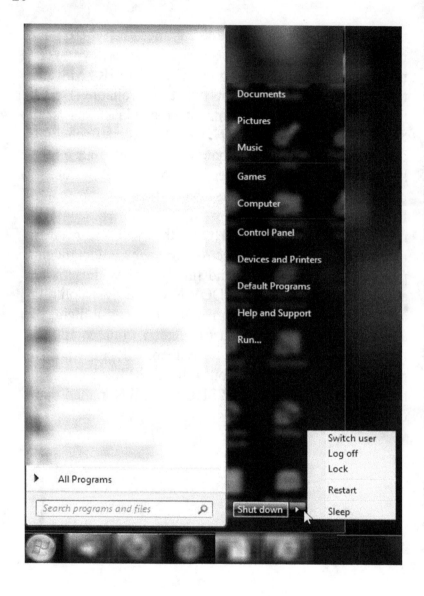

ALL PROGRAMS

From the ALL PROGRAMS button, you will be able to find all of the programs that have been installed on your computer. You will also be able to find many useful items that have been installed at the factory. Take some time to look at what you have available. You can hover over ALL PROGRAMS to expand the list or you can left click on it. You will notice some items have an icon to the left and others will have a file folder icon. Left clicking on the ones with icons will open the program associated with it. Left clicking on a folder will open a sub menu of items contained within. Left click on the ALL PROGRAMS button and look for the file folder that says ACCESSORIES. Left click on ACCESSORIES and a sub menu opens with some useful items. One that I use frequently is the CALCULATOR. Another one that is very helpful to new users is GETTING STARTED. You can see examples of these on the next pages.

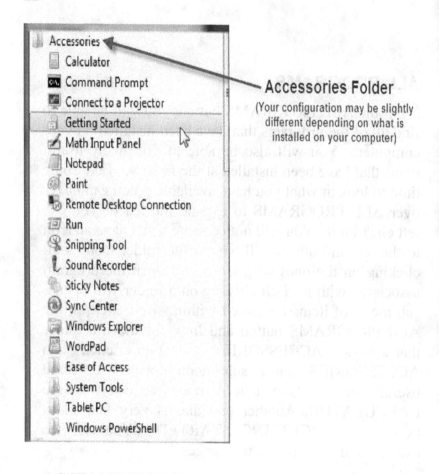

Accessories Folder

(Your configuration may be slightly different depending on what is installed on your computer)

ACCESSORIES FOLDER

Notice that some of the items have icons and some have file folders. Once again, left clicking on any of the icons will open that item and left clicking on a folder will open another sub menu.

CALCULATOR

GETTING STARTED

This is a great resource for new computer users.

PROGRAM ICONS

The program icons located in the TASK BAR show what programs are open and running on your computer. These icons provide an easy way to switch between programs you are using without having to start them each time you want to use them. Just left click on one of the icons and that program will come to the front of all other windows that are open. Left click it again and it will minimize to the task bar. Please note that even though it is convenient to have all of your programs open with easy access from the TASK BAR, the more items that are running at one time may cause your computer speed to slow down. Keep open only the ones that you are using during your computing session. Some programs you will want to use each time you start your computer. For example you may want to have quick access to INTERNET EXPLORER. Here is a quick way to permanently add programs to the TASK BAR. After you open a program or document, an icon will appear in the TASK BAR. *Right* click once on the icon and it will open a CONTEXT MENU.

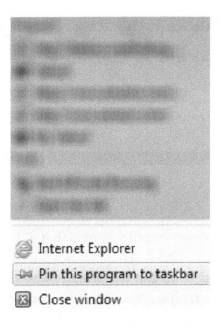

Internet Explorer

Pin this program to taskbar

Close window

Above I have opened the CONTEXT MENU for INTERNET EXPLORER. The top portion that is blurred lists some of the websites that have recently been used. Left clicking on any of those will re-open that website. The lower portion is what we are interested in. Particularly the item second from the bottom that has the push pin icon. Left click once on PIN THIS PROGRAM TO TASKBAR. You have now added this program to the TASK BAR and will be able to open it with one left click. If at any time you wish to unpin the program, just repeat the steps, and the push pin icon will now display UNPIN THIS PROGRAM FROM THE TASK BAR.

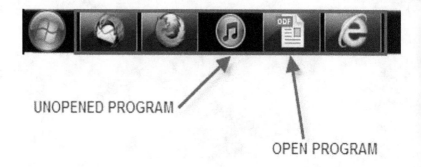

UNOPENED PROGRAM

OPEN PROGRAM

You can see in the graphic above that I have several programs on my TASK BAR. Not all of them are running, though. You can tell which ones are open and running by the translucent square over each one. Notice that the one in the middle does not have the square, much like a glass window, placed over it. That program is pinned to the TASK BAR and is ready to open at any time I wish. The others all have the translucent square over them and are running in the background. I can easily switch from one program to the next just by left clicking on any of these icons.

NOTIFICATION AREA

This area of the TASK BAR has information on your computer's current status. It shows the time and date and also if you have a current internet connection. This is also where you have quick access to your speaker volume and some important programs that run in the background. You will also notice a flag icon. This is where you will be notified of any important updates that your computer might need. You can customize the notification area by left clicking on the upward pointing arrow and selecting CUSTOMIZE.

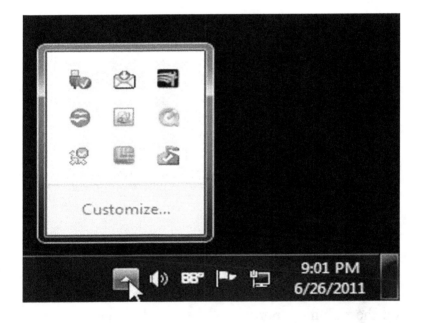

This will bring up a new window, shown on the next page, where you can customize what you see in this area.

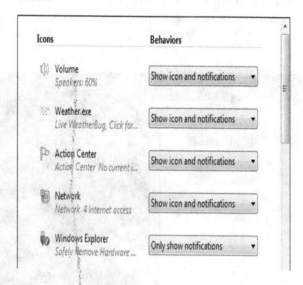

Select which icons and notifications appear on the taskbar

If you choose to hide icons and notifications, you won't be notified about changes or updates. To view hidden icons at any time, click the arrow next to the notification area on the taskbar.

Icons	Behaviors
Volume *Speakers: 60%*	Show icon and notifications
Weather.exe *Live WeatherBug, Click for...*	Show icon and notifications
Action Center *Action Center No current i...*	Show icon and notifications
Network *Network 4 Internet access*	Show icon and notifications
Windows Explorer *Safely Remove Hardware ...*	Only show notifications

SHOW DESKTOP BUTTON

This is a really fun feature of Windows 7. It is located on the rightmost portion of the task bar and is a small translucent rectangle. Find it with your mouse and let your mouse hover over it. Your open windows will all disappear and you will see your computer's desktop. Move it away and your windows will reappear. You can also left click on it to minimize all windows. This is a quick way to hide any work you have going on that you don't want others to see. This is often better than just minimizing the current window, because you may have other windows open that you would like to guard as well. One left click and your desktop will appear. When you are ready to return to your work, left click once more on the button and you will be returned to what you had open before. I find this useful if I am working on something and need to be away from the computer for just a short time and don't want to close my programs. Go ahead and try it a few times. It's great fun!

SECURITY

Before we move on to the next topic, we should make sure that you are safe while you are on the internet. You've probably heard about viruses, worms and other nasty things that can attack your computer and take over or completely disable it. There are many good computer security programs available. More than likely, your computer came with a free trial of one. After your free 60 or 90 day trial is over, you will be asked to purchase the full program to continue protection. But there are free programs that are available that are just as secure as the paid versions. I recommend that you use either AVG Free or Microsoft Security Essentials. They are both available for download and will protect your computer from threats from the internet and email. I am using Microsoft Security Essentials, but have been a long time AVG Free user. Here are the addresses for the downloads:

http://free.avg.com/us-en/homepage

http://www.microsoft.com/en-us/security_essentials/default.aspx

They are both completely free to download and use. Just left click in the address bar of your internet homepage and type in whichever address you choose, then hit enter on your keyboard. Follow the onscreen prompts to get your computer protected. Don't be alarmed if the initial scan of your computer takes quite awhile. There are a lot of files and programs that it will be checking to make sure that you haven't encountered any nasty viruses prior to installation. You can still use your computer while the scan is in progress, but it may slow things down a bit. Once the initial scan is done, you probably won't even notice it running in the background.

EMAIL

If you are going to be using a computer, chances are good that you will want to be able to use email as well. There are several different types of email clients that you can use. The two that we will focus on are graphical and web based. I like the term desktop client for the graphical email, because it is accessed from your desktop that is what I will be calling it. Just know that if this is what you use and someone suggests to you that you have a graphical email client, they are one and the same.

DESKTOP EMAIL CLIENT

Desktop email clients include, Microsoft Outlook and Mozilla Thunderbird. There are others, but these are the most widely known and used. They are programs that are installed on your computer and are accessible only (for the most part) from that computer. For this reason they are quickly falling out of favor. I use a desktop client in addition to a web based client. I use Mozilla Thunderbird on my desktop computer, and I have only one address assigned to it. Mozilla Thunderbird is a free download and is relatively easy to set up. If you are interested in obtaining it here is the download address:

http://www.mozilla.org/projects/thunderbird/

Look for the link on the page that says CURRENT

RELEASE, left click on it and follow the onscreen prompts to download.

You may have Microsoft Outlook installed on your computer as part of the Microsoft Office package. This is a great program and is very similar to Mozilla Thunderbird, but is not free. It may have come installed as part of your computer's software package. Mozilla Thunderbird was built based on the same platform as Microsoft Outlook.

With either of these desktop email clients, you will need to have an email address already assigned to you. It can be one given to you by your internet service provider, one associated with a website you operate, or it can be a web based email client address.

WEB BASED EMAIL CLIENT

There are many web based email clients to choose from. Some of the more popular include Hotmail, Yahoo Mail, AOL and Gmail. I use Gmail which is owned and supported by Google. Web based clients allow you to check your email anywhere that you have an internet connection and computer access. For this reason, they are gaining in popularity. Another reason for their popularity is that you can use different email addresses for different purposes. You can have several accounts with the same email client. Lets get started and set up a web based email using Gmail.

Open Internet Explorer. Left click in the address bar type:

Mail.google.com

Note that there is no www. preceding the address.

Hit enter on your keyboard. A new window will open.

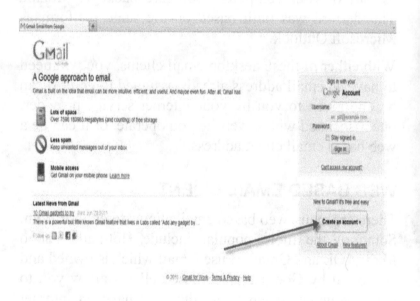

LEFT CLICK on the button that says CREATE AN ACCOUNT.

Get started with Gmail

First name:

Last name:

Desired Login Name: @gmail.com

Examples: JSmith, John.Smith

[check availability!]

Choose a password: Password strength:

Minimum of 8 characters in length.

Re-enter password:

☑ Stay signed in

☑ Enable Web History Learn More

Security question: Choose a question ...   ▾

If you forget your password we will ask for the answer to your security question. Learn More

Answer:

Recovery email:

This address is used to authenticate your account should you ever encounter problems or forget your password. If you do not have another email address, you may leave this field blank. Learn More

Location: United States   ▾

Birthday:

MM/DD/YYYY (e.g. "7/9/2011")

Word Verification: Type the characters you see in the picture below.

explists

♿

Letters are not case-sensitive

By clicking on 'I accept' below you are agreeing to the Terms of Service above and both the Program Policy and the Privacy Policy.

[I accept Create my account]

The first step is to enter your first and last name. Then you will choose your desired login name which will be followed by @gmail.com. You don't need to type that part, just the part that is in front of it. I am setting up a new email address and I put my first and last name in the first two fields. Now I am going to choose a login name. The login name must be between 6 and 30 characters. I type *computers* in the login field and left click the check availability button. That name is not available, but it gives me alternate suggestions. I can choose one of those or try another login name. This step may take some time. Try different combinations until you get one that is available that you are comfortable with. I finally stumble upon *momsguru*. After all this is a book I started for my mom.

Once you find a login name that is available, you will need to choose a password. The password must be at least 8 characters. Try to choose a combination of letters and numbers that will not be easy for anyone to guess. But also make it something that you can remember. You will need to type in your password twice, and when you do, it will be checked for strength as far as security is concerned.

Next you will choose a security question to answer. This is used to recover your password if you would happen to forget it. There is a drop down list of security questions that you can choose from, or you can write your own. Highlight the question you want to use, or the option to write your own and left click on it. If you use a question that is suggested, the next step will be to write your answer. If you write your own security question, you will type your question in the box that appears before you move on the the answer field. Make sure that you choose a question which you will remember the answer to.

The next field is for a recovery email address. You may be able to enter a work email address here, or even one of a trusted family member. My mom has one of my email addresses listed. This is for extreme cases in which you are not able to remember your password or your security question answer. If this happens, you will be able to recover your account by accessing the email that will be sent to the recovery email address.

Finally you will enter your date of birth, copy a verification word and then agree to the terms to create your email account. The verification word is used to ensure that you are a real person trying to set up this account. If you don't get the letters right the first time, you will need to re-enter your password and try again. Usually I have success at least by the second try. These verification words are not always *words,* so just type what you see even if it makes no sense. If you are having difficulty, you can left click on the wheelchair icon for additional assistance and will be given a verbal set of letters or numbers to type. When you have filled in all of the requested fields, left click the button that says I ACCEPT. CREATE MY ACCOUNT. Your next screen should be a congratulations screen.

Congratulations!

You've successfully signed up for Gmail! Here's a quick run through to help you get comfortable.

Show me my account »

Archive instead of delete
Tidy up your inbox without deleting anything. You can always search to find what you need or look in "All Mail."

Chat and video chat
Chat with your contacts directly within Gmail. You can even talk face-to-face with built-in video chat.

Labels instead of folders
Labels do the work of folders with an extra bonus: you can add more than one to an email.

© Google - Terms

Congratulations, you have set up your email. Now left click on the SHOW ME MY ACCOUNT button.

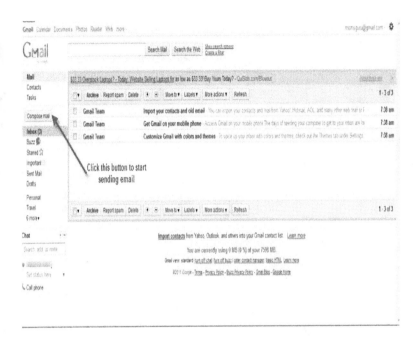

You should have already received email from the Gmail team. Left click on any one of the emails that you have received and you will be able to read it. After you have read your email, left click on the blue link above it that says BACK TO INBOX. When you are done reading any emails that interest you, go ahead and left click on the COMPOSE MAIL button. Your next screen should look something like this:

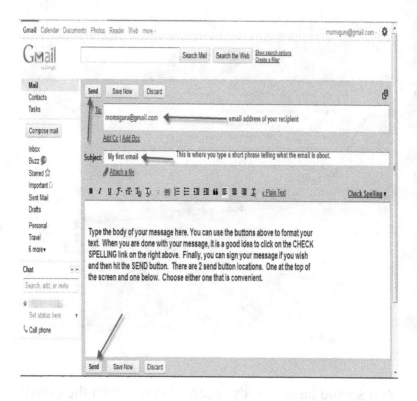

Test your email skills out by sending an email to me at *my* new email address. I would love to hear how you are doing. My new address is momsguru@gmail.com.

You will probably want to spend some time left clicking on some of the links on the left side of the Gmail window. These are like folders that you would keep in a file cabinet. INBOX is the folder where you will look to see if you have new mail to read. The SENT MAIL folder shows mail that you have sent to others. The DRAFTS folder is for mail that you have started composing but have not yet sent. Left click on any of the folders or links that you see. It won't change any of your settings, and it is easy to get back to where you started just by left clicking on the INBOX folder or the back arrow on your browser window. This is sometimes the easiest way to get an idea of what some of your programs are capable of doing for you.

CUT, COPY AND PASTE

When I first started using a computer I had a really good set of pictures, or clip art, that I wanted to use in some greeting cards that I was making to send out for the holiday's. Unfortunately, I had no idea how to get the picture from the clip art file into the program I was using for my greeting cards. So I called the help number listed with the clip art disc I had purchased to ask what I needed to do. It was simple they told me. Just copy and paste.

I didn't have a clue how to do that, so I just used the less than stellar pictures that came with my greeting card program. A few months later, one of the managers at my workplace asked me if I could show him how to copy and paste. This was a challenge that I couldn't resist. So that night at home I did some research and discovered that it really is quite easy. I have been cutting, copying and pasting ever since.

First let's define what each of the words really means when you are using a computer.

CUT

When you choose to CUT something, you will be removing it from its original location. You can CUT text or graphics from *your* documents. You cannot CUT items from web pages that you are viewing. You will use the CUT command to remove your selection and move it to another location, either in the same document or another one. This is helpful when working on text documents in which you would like to rearrange the paragraphs or sentences. You can cut an entire paragraph or page and place it in another location in your document. If you want to remove it from its location and *not* reuse it, you should use the DELETE command or keyboard key.

COPY

When you use the COPY command, you will *not* be making changes to the original document. You can use the COPY command in your own documents, and also in web pages that you are viewing since no changes will be made to the original. COPY allows you to use text or graphics from one location and copy them to another location in your document, or to a new location entirely. It is much like making a physical copy on a copy machine. The original is still intact.

PASTE

Pasting a text item or graphic is pretty much what the name implies. It allows you to take the item that you have CUT or COPIED and PASTE it in another location, either in your original document or an entirely new one. Keep in mind, though that PASTING will only place the most recent item that has been CUT or COPIED. You can also PASTE the same item repeatedly, as long as it is the last item that was CUT or

COPIED and you haven't closed your documents or powered off your computer.

When you CUT or COPY an item, it is placed in a temporary location called the clipboard. The clipboard only holds the last item that was placed there, either by CUT or COPY command. For this reason, you will need to PASTE your item before moving on to a new CUT or COPY command. Your order of operation will be either CUT then PASTE, or COPY then PASTE. Earlier versions of Windows allowed you to view the clipboard and choose which of the last several items you wished to paste. Windows 7 has done away with the viewable clipboard so that only one item is retained. In order to work around this, you might wish to open a text document or compose an email draft expressly for the purpose of saving more than one item. If you choose to go this route, you will be able to save an unlimited number of items for use at a later time. Remember the COMPOSE MAIL button in Gmail? You can paste your items into the body of an email that you never send. It will be retained in your DRAFTS folder in Gmail, which you can access at anytime and anyplace that you have an internet connection and a computer.

The process of selecting your item to CUT or COPY involves using your mouse or your keyboard as a selection tool. Find whichever one is most comfortable for you.

To use the mouse, you will need to be able to LEFT CLICK AND DRAG. You will click down on the left mouse button at the beginning of your selection.

Without releasing the button, drag the mouse to the end of your selection. Once there you will release the mouse button. Your selection should be highlighted in blue. This may take some practice but can be fun or even frustrating for the beginner. You can CLICK AND DRAG from the top to the bottom of your selection, or you can move from the bottom to the top. If you don't get all of what you want, or more that what you intended, just left click your mouse anywhere and start over.

To use the keyboard as your selection tool, you will need you place your cursor, or left click your mouse at the beginning of your selection. On the keyboard, press and hold the shift key, then use the down arrow key to reach the end of your selection. One advantage to using this method, is that as long as you keep the SHIFT KEY held down, you can adjust your selection using the up, down, right and left arrow keys. You can start at the top of your selection and move down or start at the bottom and move up.

You can use either of these methods for text document or web pages including most graphics. Once you have your selection highlighted, you are ready to CUT or COPY. Hold your mouse *without* clicking and move it until your mouse pointer is within the blue highlighted area. While in the highlighted area, ***RIGHT CLICK***. If you left click your highlight will disappear. A right click will bring up a context menu that will allow you to use the CUT or COPY command. These commands are only available when you have made a selection; on web pages only the COPY command will be available.

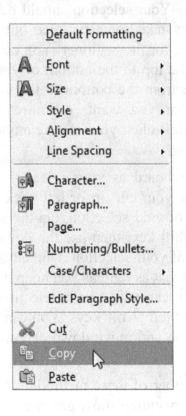

Your context menu may be slightly different than mine, but should have the CUT, COPY and PASTE commands available. Now you are ready to CUT or COPY by clicking with your LEFT mouse button. If you choose CUT, your highlighted selection will disappear. (If you didn't intend to cut and merely wanted to copy, move your mouse pointer to the beginning of where your selection would have been, RIGHT CLICK, select PASTE then LEFT CLICK. Your document should be restored.) If you choose to COPY, your selection will still be highlighted in blue. Once you have CUT or COPIED, move to the location where you want to place your selection. This can be in the same document or a new one. Find the location where you want to place your text or graphic and move the mouse pointer to that spot. RIGHT CLICK again to open the context menu. You will probably notice that since nothing has been selected in the new location, only the PASTE command is available. LEFT CLICK on PASTE and your selection will appear.

PHOTOS – DOWNLOADING AND PRINTING

Computers have changed the way we look at photographs. No longer do you have to pass a bulky album around to share your latest vacation photos – you can create a web album and share them with as many of your friends and family as you wish. You can also create albums that are available only to you or the users of your computer. You can use a favorite picture as your computer wallpaper, create a slide show, email or print photos right from your computer. And getting pictures onto your computer from your camera or memory card is easier than you might think.

Most newer computers and printers have a slot dedicated to memory card use. If no slot is available, you can transfer pictures using a USB cord attached to your camera. Most memory cards will be either an SD (Secure Digital) or xD (eXtreme Digital).

Take a look at the area of your computer where you would insert a CD, DVD or USB cable. There may be a horizontal or vertical slot labeled SD/XD. This is where you will insert your memory card. If you don't find one on your computer, check your printer to see if one is available there. Most printers that are advertised as Photo Printers will have one included. If you don't have a memory card slot in your computer or printer, use the USB cable that came with your camera.

Insert your memory card in the slot that you located. Place the card with the printed side on top and gently push it in. If you notice resistance, flip the card over and try it that way. When the card is inserted, you will be able to view or download the pictures.

After inserting the card, you will probably have an Auto Play window pop up that looks something like the one above. You have a few options to choose from which will be listed under PICTURES OPTIONS. If you have any photo editing software installed, you will be given the option to import or download your pictures using that software. You should also have the option import or download pictures using Windows. GENERAL OPTIONS lets you open the folder to view the pictures without having to make a decision yet as to whether you want to download them.

Left clicking on the tab OPEN FOLDER TO VIEW FILES will open the location where the computer is currently storing the pictures. In this case, they are still on the memory card, which on my computer is Drive F.

The left panel above shows a map of my computer. By left clicking on REMOVABLE DISK (F:), I can preview all the pictures that are available by left clicking ONCE on each file in the NAME column. The lower portion of the screen, which is shown on the next page, contains information unique to each picture. You can add tags and names in this area.

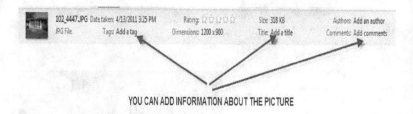

YOU CAN ADD INFORMATION ABOUT THE PICTURE

You can edit, print or upload pictures to a web album by using the FILE menu at the top of the page, or you can RIGHT CLICK on the file name to access these options in a CONTEXT MENU.

File	Edit	View	Tools	Help

Edit

Print

Set as desktop background

Preview

Open

Upload to Web Albums...

Rotate clockwise

Rotate counterclockwise

Scan with Microsoft Security Essentials...

Open with ▶

Print with KODAK AiO Home Center

Snagit ▶

Share with ▶

Send to ▶

New ▶

Snagit ▶

Snagit ▶

Snagit ▶

Create shortcut

Delete

Rename

Properties

Close

Using the OPEN FOLDER TO VIEW FILES option is a quick way to see if you want to save them to the computer, a CD, print them or even delete them. Below the menu bar is a set of quick links for printing or burning a CD.

Only the highlighted files will print or burn to your CD. Select the files you want by using the SHIFT or CRTL buttons. To select all files or a continuous set of files, hold down the SHIFT key on your keyboard and LEFT CLICK on the first file and then the last file that you want. All files selected should be highlighted in blue. You can then left click on the BURN or PRINT button. To select random files, press and hold down the CRTL button on your keyboard, then select each file by LEFT CLICKING on the file name. As you click the file name, it should highlight in blue. When you have selected your files you can print or burn them to a CD.

You can choose to save or import your pictures to your computer using the IMPORT PICTURES AND

VIDEOS USING WINDOWS option. Left clicking on that option will open a small window.

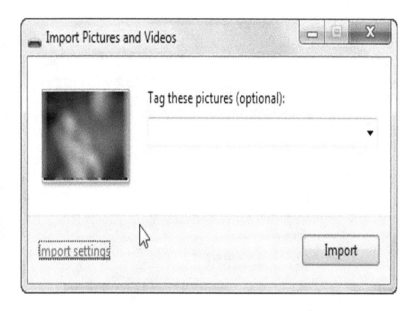

Left click on the blue IMPORT SETTINGS link.

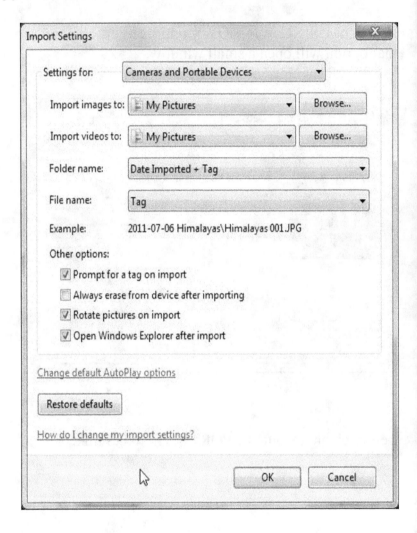

Here you can select where you want to save your pictures. I recommend using the MY PICTURES location and choosing a file name that will give a clue to the photos inside – VEGAS VACATION 2011, OUR

NEW HOME, MY FLOWER GARDEN, etc. You can name your folder anything you like that will help you know what is included. If you are satisfied with your settings, left click OK and then left click IMPORT on the next window. Your pictures will be saved to the location you specified.

To view your photographs, left click on the START BUTTON then on the PICTURES link. Choose which folder you want to see, and DOUBLE LEFT CLICK on that folder.

In the address bar, you can see that I am in the PICTURE library, and I chose the folder GRAND-DOGS. You can RIGHT CLICK on any of the pictures to open a CONTEXT MENU. A few of things you will be able to do from here are EDIT, PRINT, RENAME or SET AS DESKTOP BACKGROUND. You can choose any of the actions from the CONTEXT MENU by LEFT CLICKING on the link. Renaming your photos is not necessary, but can be extremely helpful.

This is a CONTEXT MENU opened by RIGHT CLICKING on a picture.

LEFT CLICK on any of the items to perform that action.

LEFT CLICK on the SEND TO link to bring up another menu. Here you can email your photos to friends and family.

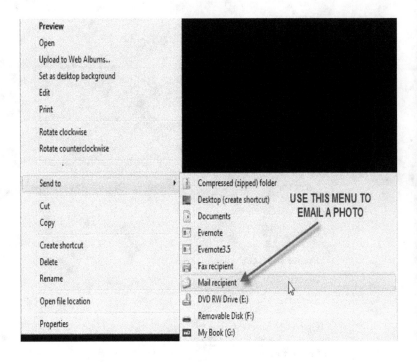

PHOTOS – EDITING

When you start viewing your photographs, many will need to be edited for color or balance or to remove that pesky red eye. Your camera may have come with photo editing software and there are many programs that you can purchase that can do amazing things. If you are not a professional photographer, I suggest that you use one of the many free programs available. The open source equivalent to Photoshop is Gimp, a free image manipulation program. You can download it at http://www.gimp.org. Kodak makes Easyshare Software that is available to download at http://www.kodak.com. Not surprisingly, Google also makes a free software called Picasa. Download it at http://picasa.google.com. I like using Picasa simply because they have a button on the editor called I'M FEELING LUCKY. Choose a picture to edit, left click on the I'M FEELING LUCKY button, and you can see the changes immediately. If you are happy with the changes, simply return to your library to view and edit more pictures. If you wish you hadn't made the changes, left click on the UNDO I'M FEELING LUCKY BUTTON. All of the editing that you do has the option of being undone before you save the final version. Picasa also has a great feature for tagging faces in your pictures. Tag a few faces and Picasa will scan the faces in other pictures and suggest matches. It is surprising how often it is correct.

PHOTOS – SETTING UP A WEB ALBUM

Now that you have all of your favorite photographs saved to your computer, you will probably want to be able to view them from other computer locations and share whole albums with family and friends. Having your photos saved to a web album will allow you to view them from any internet connected computer.

In an earlier section, we set up a web based email account using Gmail. Open up your web browser and navigate to Gmail. LEFT CLICK your INTERNET EXPLORER shortcut on the TASKBAR. Your home page will open. In the address bar, type mail.google.com and hit enter on your keyboard. If you are not signed in automatically, left click in the box to enter your USERNAME and PASSWORD, then left click to sign in. At the top of the Gmail window are links to other Google applications. Left click on PHOTOS to open Google's Picasa Web Albums. You can sign in here using your Gmail address and password. Once you are signed in you can create your profile and add photographs.

Left click on the Photos link and then UPLOAD NEW
PHOTOS. In the new window that opens, left click on
the LAUNCH PICASA button. You will then be able to
add photographs, name your album and adjust your
privacy settings. You can choose which albums you
want to share and with whom.

APPENDIX 1

QUICK CLICK START GUIDE

SETTING UP YOUR HOME PAGE

Left click START BUTTON, Left click INTERNET EXPLORER ICON, In address bar, type web address, press Enter on the keyboard, Left click TOOLS, Left click INTERNET OPTIONS, Left click USE CURRENT, Left click APPLY, Left click OK.

ADDING FAVORITES

While on a favorite website, Left click FAVORITES on toolbar, Left click ADD TO FAVORITES, rename if needed, Left click OK

SHORTCUTS AND THE TASKBAR

When a program is open, RIGHT CLICK on the PROGRAM ICON on the TASKBAR. Left click PIN THIS PROGRAM TO TASKBAR. The icon on the taskbar will open the program with one LEFT CLICK in the future.

START BUTTON AND ALL PROGRAMS

LEFT CLICK on the START BUTTON, LEFT CLICK on ALL PROGRAMS. Navigate to any program or folder and LEFT CLICK TO OPEN.

SECURITY

Install a free virus protection program.

http://free.avg.com/us-en/homepage

http://www.microsoft.com/en-us/security_essentials/default.aspx

EMAIL

Use a Desktop email client such as Microsoft Outlook or Mozilla Thunderbird if you already have an email address assigned to you.

http://www.mozilla.org/projects/thunderbird/

Use a Web based email client such as Hotmail, Yahoo Mail or Gmail to create your own email address and have access at any internet connected computer.

Mail.google.com

CUT, COPY AND PASTE

Highlight selection by LEFT CLICKING and DRAGGING. RIGHT CLICK in selected area then LEFT CLICK on CUT to remove selection from its current location. LEFT CLICK on COPY to keep selection in its current location. Once the selection is either CUT or COPIED, navigate to the location where you want to place the selection. RIGHT CLICK then LEFT CLICK on PASTE.

PHOTOS -DOWNLOADING AND PRINTING

Locate the the SD or xD slot on your computer or printer. Insert your memory card or insert your camera's connected USB cord. From the AUTO PLAY menu, choose by left clicking to OPEN FOLDER TO VIEW FILES using WINDOWS EXPLORER or IMPORT PICTURES AND VIDEOS using WINDOWS EXPLORER. RIGHT CLICK on any picture to EDIT, PRINT or UPLOAD TO WEB ALBUM. Select pictures to burn on CD or print by using the SHIFT or CRTL button on your keyboard and LEFT CLICKING from first to last using the SHIFT key, or random selections by LEFT CLICKING and holding down the CRTL key.

PHOTOS – EDITING

Use a purchased or free PHOTO EDITING SOFTWARE to make changes or to enhance photos and remove red eye.

http://www.kodak.com

http://picasa.google.com

http://www.gimp.org/

PHOTOS – SETTING UP A WEB ALBUM

Log into your Gmail account and left click on the PHOTO link located at the upper portion of the window. Create a Picasa account using your Gmail email address and password. Left click on UPLOAD NEW PHOTOS and LAUNCH PICASA. Create your user profile, add photos and adjust your security settings to define who you will share your albums with.

APPENDIX 2

POPULAR WEBSITES

NEWS AND SEARCH

www.msn.com

www.yahoo.com

www.aol.com

www.google.com

www.foxnews.com

www.cnn.com

AUCTION AND SHOPPING SITES

www.amazon.com

www.ebay.com

www.etsy.com

www.craigslist.org

REASEARCH

www.wikipedia.org

www.ancestry.com

www.usgenweb.org

SOCIAL NETWORKING AND ENTERTAINMENT

www.pogo.com

www.facebook.com

www.twitter.com

www.youtube.com

MUSIC

www.pandora.com

www.itunes.com

PRODUCTIVITY

www.openoffice.org

www.lifehacker.com

*BE SURE TO LOOK FOR MORE MOM'S GURU
GUIDES COMING SOON*